The Bare Bones
Weekend Biz Plan

Copyright © 2011 by Ellen Rohr

Bare Bones Business Books may be purchased for business or promotional use or for special sales. For sales information or permissions to reprint the this text or the material within, contact the publisher at:

Bare Bones Business Publishing
3120 S. Know It All Lane
Rogersville, MO 65472
877.629.7647

www.barebonesbiz.com

ISBN: 978-0-9845876-3-6
Printed in the U.S.A.

The Bare Bones
Weekend Biz
Plan

Launch a Profitable Business by Monday

by Ellen Rohr

FROM BRIGHT IDEA TO BIG BUCKS – HOW TO START A PROFITABLE BUSINESS OVER A WEEKEND!

*"Knowledge of what is possible is
the beginning of happiness."*

~ George Santayana

Perhaps you've got a great idea for a business...or

...You are ready to take your job and shove it...or

...You have a business already, and it's sucking the life out of you!

Here's what you can do: Over the course of a weekend, you can put your business together. You can clarify your vision and assemble a simple Biz Plan for making it happen. Profitably. Without draining your time and energy for no real reward. Without creating a pile of debt.

I've laid out an exact agenda. From Friday evening to Sunday evening, I have put together a path that will guide you through the process of clarifying your vision for your ideal business. Then, you commit to aligned action that will help you create that ideal business. And, you can hit the ground running on Monday.

You could take a little longer than a weekend. Once upon a time, I wrote a terrific book called "The Bare Bones Biz Plan." In this book, I help you through the business planning process. Over the course of six weeks, you can work through the daily exercises and assemble your Biz Plan Binder.

Lately, I've been wondering...how could you jump start a stalled business quickly? How could you "strike while the iron is hot" with a new business idea? How fast could you move from frustration to focused action?

THAT is what inspired me to create an agenda for putting a business plan together in one weekend. So, you don't have to get your business plan done in a weekend. But...you could! Why not give it a go? Why not follow this agenda?

Now, you don't have to follow a strict agenda like this. I will take care of the details for you. You don't have to waste time thinking about that. Try allowing yourself to be helped this way. Try stretching yourself. Being a bit uncomfortable can be a powerful way to expand your boundaries and realize your potential.

Because you are reading this, you have the desire to be successful. The more clarity you have about what you want, the greater your desire becomes. The desire drives the willingness. If you are willing to do what it takes to create a successful, profitable business, you will find a way. This *Weekend Biz Plan* approach is a simpler, easier way than racing forward without any structure.

One of the reasons I wrote a business planning book is because so many people approach me with a rapid fire description of what they want to do for a business. But I can't get my head around it and their words are all over the place. So, I ask, "What have you got written down? What can you show me?" At that point they usually just point to their head. "It's all in here." Well, moving the ideas to paper, to a Binder, to your iPad or computer, is the start of making it real. Thought begets reality. Thought moves to material form by writing it or typing it.

Why not clear out a weekend and follow this game plan? Prove that you can take charge of your time and commit to 48 hours of focused thought and action. If you can pull that off, you will increase your confidence that you can make sweeping changes in your life. That's a powerful feeling. This weekend, you could take a quantum leap in your life and in your business.

Commit to a weekend in the next month. Write in on your Calendar. (In blood?) And communicate to all who may come looking for you that you will be on a retreat and unavailable. Arrange to have dependant family members depend on someone else for the weekend. Yes. Yes, you can do this.

Here's your agenda for the weekend:

AGENDA

From Bright Idea to Big Bucks – how to start a profitable business over a weekend!

Friday evening

Saturday

7:30 A.M.

8:30 A.M.

9:30 A.M.

10:30 A.M.

11:30 A.M.

....

TIP: Follow my lead and stick to the agenda as best you can. If you don't finish an exercise in the time alloted, no worries! Move on the the next one. Your Biz Plan is never done. And you'll never do any of it wrong! Does that make you feel better? Great! The Biz Plan is all about helping you gain a clearer vision of what you want your business–and life–to be. And, help you commit to some action that will move you toward that. Easy!

FRIDAY EVENING

Gather Your Supplies

Go to the Office Supply Store

(Or check your office for the following items):

- A one-inch three ring binder. Get a nice one. Your Biz Plan is going inside.

- A hundred sheets of paper. (You can create a few drafts of each exercise.)
- A single subject, three hole, spiral bound notebook. This will be your Master To Do List.
- A small package of 3″ by 3″ sticky notes.

Note that you could create your Biz Plan on your laptop, or your iPad. Whatever works for you. I like the Binder and the iPad versions because you want to make the Biz Plan easily accessible and demonstrable. For instance, if you found yourself sitting next to Warren Buffet on an airplane, could you easily whip out your Biz Plan and go through it with him? That could be a "readiness meets opportunity" moment for you.

Go to the supermarket:

Stock up on food for the weekend. Like…

- Cereal, yogurt, fruit for breakfast
- Bagged salad and hearty bread for lunch
- Roaster chicken, mac and cheese, quesadillas or soup and crackers for dinner
- Nuts, granola, dried fruit for snacks

The idea is to have simple, healthy food at the ready so that you can prep and eat without a lot of fuss.

Depending on what your supermarket carries, you may be able to get everything on the Office Supply list at the supermarket. One stop shopping.

Go to www.BareBonesBiz.com/weekend and download forms:

We stored all the simple forms you'll need to complete the exercises throughout the weekend. Visit the site and "Save" the forms to your computer. Start a folder called Weekend Biz Plan and save the forms there, so they are ready for tomorrow. You can print them up or you can edit the Word docs and Excel spreadsheets directly as you work through the exercises.

Get your head cleaned out:

Before bed, meditate for 10 minutes. Set the alarm for the morning. I suggest 6:30 am. Get to bed in time to get 8 hours of sleep. (Don't need or like that much sleep? Adjust the schedule accordingly.) Right before you turn in, find a comfortable chair in a quiet spot. Try this meditation technique…

- Set the timer, or your phone alarm, for 10 minutes. Collect your attention into the middle of your head. Pull your thoughts away from the past or the future and try to focus on right here, right now.

- ◉ Focus on your breathing. If you are not an experienced meditation practitioner, your mind will wander. Don't fret. Just bring your attention back to the center of your head. Relax, and discover your breathing.

- ◉ When the timer goes off, go to bed. Sleep well and sweet dreams.

- ◉ If you wake up in the middle of the night, silently declare your intention to go back to sleep. Try the meditation technique while lying in bed. I don't think about things in the dark. Practice clearing your mind of thoughts. Collect your attention in the center of your head. Keep returning to the here and now and let thoughts go.

This is an important part of the weekend. Your ability to let go of old thoughts, "taped" patterns of thinking is essential to creating a successful business. Thought begets reality. Think new thoughts and take inspired, new action…and you will create a different outcome. You can make your dreams come true. It requires that you take charge of what is going on between your ears. Perhaps you have spent a lifetime defining and limiting yourself. Perhaps you have let others impose their limitations on you. The point of power is right now. You can create a better reality. New thoughts and aligned action are what it takes. As you engage in business planning over this weekend, the intention is to discover what you really want and move in that direction.

Don't fret if this meditation exercise is challenging. The first dozen times I tried to meditate, I couldn't keep from thinking about the future or the past for more than a second or two at a time. It takes practice. Just keep bringing yourself back to the here and now.

"See" you in the morning!

The structure of the weekend is intentional. You don't have to spend energy deciding what to do when. Just do this. Do it when and as suggested. The freedom is in the exercises. Focus your attention on the important things and let the structure support that. Don't over think this. Sure, you could tweak the agenda. Don't. Just do as directed and see what happens.

"You can be right. Or you can be rich."

~Wayne Dyer

SATURDAY

6:30   Rise and shine! Clean up…shower or bathe, and put on some comfy clothes. No newspaper or radio or TV. Don't allow the "real" world to influence you. If it's a real emergency someone will find you. (If you are responsible for small kids, the exception is the sitter's call. Take that one.)

7:00   Breakfast. Read a page or two from an inspirational book. Like *Think and Grow Rich* or *The Power of Positive Thinking*.

7:20   10 minutes of meditation. Meditating helps stop the "monkey mind" obsessive thoughts that keep us locked in our current conditions. As the song goes, "Free your mind and the rest will follow."

"There is nothing like a dream to create the future."

~ Victor Hugo

7:30 A.M.

One Hour to Describe Your Perfect Life

Yes, this is a guide for planning a business. However, the reality is that there is NO separation between business and the rest of your life. Your business is an aspect of your life and needs to align with what you want to be, do and have.

Sure, you want more...or enough...or something different from what you now have. Now, get more specific. What *exactly* do you want?

Write down your Perfect Life. Ask yourself, "What do I want?" and listen for the very first thoughts that come to mind. Write them down without judgment. Notice your feelings as you write the words on the Perfect Life form. Did you save the forms you will need for the *Weekend Biz Plan* already? Great. (If not, ind it at www.barebonesbiz.com/weekend) Find the Perfect Life form. Start writing! If it feels good you are on the right track. If it feels good, you are on the right track.

Start with when you wake up, and move through each hour of the day. Jot down thoughts and descriptions of what the Perfect Life would be like. How would you spend it? With whom? Where? Would you work? What does your company look like? How many people? How much money would you make? How much time would you spend with your family?

Contemplate how a business fits into your Perfect Life. What does it look like, smell like, feel like? What kind of work do you do? Who are your customers? How much time would you spend in your business? What hours would you work, ideally? Find pictures that capture how you see this business. Incorporate business elements into your Perfect Life.

Write it all down. This is your Perfect Life. Three hole punch the pages and store your Perfect Life in your *Biz Plan Binder*.

Spend up to an hour on this exercise. You can come back to it another day, and you can add to it or revise it as your understanding of what you want gains clarity. This exercise may come easily to you, or you may find this the most challenging work you have ever done. Seek to find your authentic desires. Honor that which you want, because your unique gifts and talents are found there. Relax in the understanding that when you focus on these gifts and talents, you will find ways to share them.

☐ When you are finished, read what you wrote and look over the pictures. Then give thanks that these things are manifesting for you.

8:30 A.M.

One Hour to Write The Mission

"Before you decide on what, ask why."

~ Simon Sinek

I f the WHY is big enough, it will give you the courage and strength to follow through with your business plan. It will also provide support for *the rest of your Biz Plan.* Your Mission Statement answers the question, "Why should this business exist?" and is the cornerstone of your business.

Mission Statement Exercise

Find inspiration in your Perfect Life exercise. Also consider the BIG IDEA or moment of epiphany that may have inspired you to start your business.

Spend an hour thinking about WHY you are in business. Too often, the day-to-day demands on our time and energy keep us from thinking about the things that really matter. When you are thinking, it doesn't look like you are doing anything! Rest assured that thinking is the highest-level work you can do.

Ask these questions, think, and write down your thoughts...

- ☉ Why should my business exist?
- ☉ What excites me about it?

- How does my company impact people, communities, countries, and the planet?
- What would be lost without my business?
- What would be gained without my business?
- What inspired me to start my business?
- What's the point?

Distill the thoughts you have written until you can summarize your Mission Statement. Keep it simple and focused. Read your Mission Statement out loud several times and commit it to memory.

Don't worry about coming up with the right Mission Statement. Trust that by asking these questions, you will discover your business Mission. The *Weekend Biz Plan* is a flexible, living, growing plan. As you grow and change, you can come back to this page and revise and refine your Mission. Write down what rings true for you now. Edit it down to 25 words or less. Any longer and you dilute the power of it. Use the Mission Statement form…found at www.barebonesbiz.com/weekend

☐ Three hole punch the page and put it in your *Biz Plan Binder*.

Good work! Note that even if you are not finished with these exercises put SOMETHING down and move on to the next one. You may find that your first thoughts and words are the best ones. In any event, you can always "plus" your Biz Plan later. Write something and press on!

TIP! Not finished with the Mission Statement exercise? No problem. Whatever you have written is a good start. Leave it be...and move on to the next exercise. This advice applies to all the exercises. Just take a swing at each exercise and move on when the time is up. This process is powerful and you will have a working Biz Plan by the end of the Weekend. It won't be done...however, it's never done! You will continue to review and refine your Biz Plan–and business–beyond this weekend.

So...relax and enjoy the process!

TIME FOR A BREAK!

Eat something healthy while you listen to some music. Close your eyes for a few minutes. Meditate. Take a few deep breaths. Enjoy knowing that you are rockin' this business planning process and your Perfect Life is on its way.

9:30 A.M.

One Hour to Prepare Your Elevator Speech

"Boldness in business is the first, second and third thing."

~ Thomas Fuller

The first part of this exercise is to answer this question, what makes your company different and better than others that aim to satisfy the same customer needs or deliver a similar product or service? This is called your Unique Selling Proposition, your USP.

Avoid settling on a USP that identifies you as the low-cost provider. That is a brutal USP, because you lose your advantage every time a competing company lowers its price. Instead, focus on what makes you smarter, faster, kinder, cleaner, better-smelling, more convenient, less confusing, easier to work with, more committed, more fun, uniquely qualified to serve your customers.

What makes you different and better? Jot down your answer or answers. Next, work the USP into a short, attention-getting statement. It's called an Elevator Speech.

The Elevator Speech

Real Estate Sales Trainer Bernard Zick taught me how to create an Elevator Speech. The term "Elevator Speech" is inspired by the time spent with a stranger in an elevator. During the time it takes to get from one floor to the next, what could you say that would cause a person to perceive a need…and understand that you are the one to solve it?

The Elevator Speech format goes like this:

- ⊙ "You know how…?" Hit them with their problem/challenge/heart's desire.
- ⊙ "What we do is…" Fix it. Tell them what you do to solve that problem/help overcome that challenge/deliver their heart's desire. Include your USP.

Be creative! This format is flexible and designed to help you get started on your Elevator Speech. You'll know you have a winning Elevator Speech when the response is, "That's interesting! Tell me more."

Elevator Speeches are useful! It's great to have a snappy reply to the standard question, "So what do you do?" You can write a few Elevator Speeches. As you use them, you can refine them…or customize depending on to whom you are talking. Have fun…with this. It's a powerful way to start a conversation and spread the word about your business.

- ☐ Use the form at www.barebonesbiz.com/weekend called Elevator Speech and put the page in your *Biz Plan Binder*.

Note how these exercises "dovetail" with each other. Feel free to return to a previous exercise and edit it as you refine your thoughts in a new exercise.

Next up…setting Goals!

10:30 A.M.

45 Minutes to Set Your Goals

Goals are "to have" statements. Goals are what you want to have from your company. Goals are measurable and achievable.

Look over your Plan Binder. Review your Mission. Now set a timer for 20 minutes and start writing! Write down any ideas, to do's and projects that will move you closer to your Mission and your Vision. Don't judge, just write.

When the 20 minutes are up, go through the list. Identify 20 items that will have the most impact on achieving your Mission…and just be fun and motivating to you.

Craft those items into Goal statements:

To have_____by _____.

Include growth and profitability Goals. Don't buy into the myth that if you do what you love, the money will follow. It may not! Confront your money hang-ups. Money is not at odds with living life at the highest spiritual level. Money is just a medium for exchanging energy. Understand that money is the lifeblood of your business. Without it, you'll be out of business and lose a wonderful way to be of service.

Put your Goals to the test. Are they achievable and measurable? Have you committed to the due date? Use numbers, dollars, percentages and hours to clarify your Goals.

Use the form called Goals at www.barebonesbiz.com/weekend and put your Goals in your *Biz Plan Binder*. For goals that don't make it to

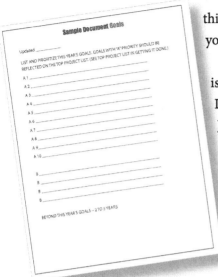

Sample Document Goals

Updated _____

LIST AND PRIORITIZE THIS YEAR'S GOALS. GOALS WITH "A" PRIORITY SHOULD BE
REFLECTED ON THE TOP PROJECT LIST. (SEE TOP PROJECT LIST IN GETTING IT DONE.)

A 1 _____
A 2 _____
A 3 _____
A 4 _____
A 5 _____
A 6 _____
A 7 _____
A 8 _____
A 9 _____
A 10 _____

B _____
B _____
B _____
B _____

BEYOND THIS YEAR'S GOALS – 2 TO 5 YEARS

this year's list, store them on a page in your Master To +++++Do list.

Note that the *Weekend Biz Plan* is designed to be fun, fast and easy. Don't sweat what you put down. Just do it! You can go back later. A Biz Plan is never done. You can't do this wrong. If you are stressing about an exercise, just put something down…and move on. Trust that your first response to the exercises is valid. And if you are not finished by 11:15, put the Biz Plan down and take a break.

"Imagination is more important than knowledge."

~Albert Einstein

QUICK BREAK!

Give yourself a pat on the back! Good work on the Biz Plan so far! Now, get moving and get your blood flowing…

- ⊙ Walk around the block.
- ⊙ Play fetch with the dog.
- ⊙ Do 20 pushups and 100 jumping jacks.
- ⊙ S-T-R-E-T-C-H!
- ⊙ Run up and down the stairs.

And, jump back into business planning. Sure, you may be a bit tired or distracted or frustrated…or whatever. Thinking is high level work. You are creating an empire, a fortune and the lifestyle you really, really want. This is BIG. No turning back now. Go go go!

> TIP: Have you fallen behind on the exercises? Don't sweat it. As a wise woman once told me, "You'll never get it done. And there is no wrong in any of it." Just recharge…and charge back to your Biz Plan.

11:30 A.M.

1 Hour to Plot the Organizational Chart

For this exercise, you will need...

- The Excel sheet called Sample Organization Chart. Find it at www.barebonesbiz.com/weekend
- A blank wall or dry-erase board
- A stack of Sticky notes...the 3-by-3-inch size is good.

Start by reviewing the basic company divisions on the Sample Organization Chart. The divisions are indicated by the double-lined boxes. Do the divisions reflect the main areas of activity in your company? Customize as needed. You can use the Weekend Biz language for the divisions or substitute your own names.

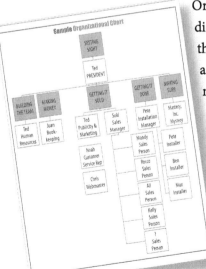

Identify Responsibilities

Use Sticky notes to identify the divisions on your Organization Chart. Put them up on the dry-erase board.

On additional Stickys, list the Responsibilities for each division.

Responsibilities are WHAT needs to be DONE to realize your Mission and achieve your Goals.

27

Arrange the Stickys to show the reporting relationships. Who is dependent on whom? Who reports to whom? Don't be bound by what is currently happening in your company. Think more broadly. Think in terms of how the company should ideally operate. Plan for growth.

Assign names to the Positions.

Put your name at the top. You are the leader. Understand that the Organization Chart flows uphill. If there is an empty Position, the person who holds the Position above it is responsible for handling that Position.

You may hold more than one Position. In a small company, each team member may hold a few Positions. You may want to outsource one or more Positions. If you do, put that company's name in the box. On the Sample Organization Chart, notice that Mastery, Inc., handles mystery shopping services.

As the company grows and as you hire more people, you can change the Position assignments. Add an additional box on the Organization Chart if more than one person is assigned to a Position.

Draw your Organization Chart (or edit the Excel form) and write in names for the Positions. Insert a copy of your Organization Chart in your *Biz Plan Binder*.

BREAK FOR LUNCH

Find a nice, comfortable place to eat in a room with a view. Eat something healthy. Don't turn on the TV.

If you must – call and check in with those who really need to hear from you. (Baby sitter? Parents? Kids?) Ignore everyone else. This time is for YOU and you don't want to risk getting off course. Instead, think about this developing business. Picture yourself in your Perfect Life… imagine what you would be doing, wearing, eating, talking to, thinking about, planning for, enjoying!

"What you think about comes about."

~ Mark Victor Hansen

Watch for thoughts that creep in, and try to burst the bubble. You want to live in that bubble! Replace those thoughts with what you really, really want. Allow yourself to think as BIG as you can…and assume that every bit of it is possible.

"Who wants a dream this is near-fetched?"

~ Howard Schultz, Chairman of Starbucks

1 P.M.

2 Hours to Draft the Financial Plan

Now it's time to address the MONEY! Find the Budget at <u>www. barebonesbiz.com/weekend</u> Click through it and see how it is set up. This is a super simple way for you to consider your expenses and what you will need in sales to cover them and leave your intended profit. A Budget also helps you come up with a reasonable Selling Price strategy. Nice!

Basic Budgeting Steps

Start plugging in numbers for sales and expenses. The end result should be a "pretend" Income Statement that lists your Goals for sales and expenses for a future time period.

- ⊙ **Enter the dollar amounts.** Work your way down the list of expenses. Reference your Income Statement, tax returns and check register to see how much you have spent on expenses in the past. Enter an amount that seems reasonable.

- ⊙ **Fill in the sales line last.** Fill in all your projected costs, and then see how much you will need in sales to cover costs and leave your desired profit. Remember…the budget is pretend. Try a couple different scenarios, with different assumptions for sales and expenses.

- ⊙ **Play the "what if" game.** Do several versions of your budget. Save each budget with a different file name so that you can reference each one. Creating monthly budgets allows you to better predict sales and profitability. Is your business typically busier in the holiday season? Reflect that in your budget. Are you considering a booth at a local trade show? Increase marketing costs in your budget for that month.

- ⊙ **Think like a watermelon.** It only takes one seed to grow a watermelon plant. One plant can generate a dozen watermelons. Each watermelon is filled with hundreds of seeds. Theoretically, it only takes one seed to carry on the watermelon family. But Nature knows that "stuff happens" and plans for abundance. Do the same for your budget. Put a little cushion in the numbers.

- ⊙ **The budget should show a profit!** Sales minus expenses should be a positive number. You may choose to create a short-term loss while you build your company. For instance, you may incur expenses before your company opens for business. The best approach is to budget for profitability every month.

- ⊙ **Keep a Budgeting Log.** You are going to pull some of your budgeted numbers from thin air. Write down your reasoning as you are coming up with the numbers for your budget. When you refer to your budget in the months to come, you may forget your assumptions. Write them down on a page in your Master to do list. Or, type them up. Call the page Budgeting Log and store it in your *Biz Plan Binder*.

"I do everything for a reason. Most of the time the reason is money."

~ Dorothy Parker

BRIEF BREAK!

From 3:00 to 3:15 try and STRETCH out every muscle in your body, from head to toe and finger tip to finger tip. Your amazing spine can move in six directions. Explore!

Back to the Biz Plan...

Business without profit is not business anymore than a pickle is candy."

~ Charles F. Abbot

3:30 P.M.

1.5 Hours to Check Your Budget & Explore Pricing

"Nothing happens until something is sold."

~ "Red' Motley

When you have put your budget together, give yourself a pat on the back. Now...let's check your work. Does your budget fit in with the rest of the work you have done building your *Biz Plan Binder* and assembling your business plan?

Does the budget support your Mission and move you toward your Perfect Life? Look over your list of Goals. Is the sales line of the budget in agreement with what you wrote on your Goals list? If not, adjust one or the other...or both.

Review and refine the forms in your *Biz Plan Binder*. Make adjustments. Adjust the sales line on your budget to ensure that sales minus expenses delivers your Goal for profits.

Pricing Exercise

A useful formula for creating your selling price is this: Divide your sales Goal by the number of widgets you can sell. That's your selling price per widget. For service work, divide your sales Goal by the number of hours, or days, you can sell. That's your selling price per hour, or per day, of service time.

Refer to your budget and crunch the numbers. *The Budget* will automatically calculate your selling price per hour of service time. Explore the Key Numbers tab on the Budget. You can also play out different computations with pencil and paper.

Let's look at a simple example. Suppose your budgeted monthly sales Goal is $22,000. On average, one month has 22 days of available work time…days available to sell and deliver your goods and services.

$22,000 divided by 22 days = $1,000

So, that's your daily Sales goal.

Note that this is just a simplified example! You need to crunch the numbers for YOUR business to come up with a reasonable selling price. Also, note that this selling price will work IF the rest of the expenses and percentages fall in line. And IF the Salespeople are able to close enough calls. As you move forward with your business, you'll check your performance weekly. You can make adjustments to your budget, your pricing, your business plan, as needed.

Spend some time today working through several pricing strategies for your company. You'll probably discover that your selling price needs to be higher… maybe a lot higher…than your competition. They may not know better because they don't look at their financial reports. They may be deeply in debt or going out of business. Calculate your selling price from your budget, and include dollars for debt reduction. Don't copy your competition!

To compete with lower priced competitors, you'll have to get creative. Business is a lot more fun when you are willing to charge more than it costs.

Leverage Your USP.

The Selling Price exercise points out the importance of selling value, not low price. You can become so much better than your competitors at what you do and how you do it that your clients will be happy to pay your prices.

Leverage Your Time with Products and Information.

If your business is limited to skilled services, you are going to have to charge enough money per hour to cover all expenses and make a profit. Your skills are valuable and your time is limited. Let your budget be your guide and price accordingly.

Is there a way to deliver what you do or know without offering your time? Consider writing what you know and selling that information in books, magazines or on the Internet. Can you create a DVD or videotape that teaches others how to do the wonderful things that you do? Can you develop a product line that supports your services?

Most business owners never put any thought into their pricing! Most of them call their competitors, assume a fake voice, ask how much they charge…then charge just about the same thing. Most small businesses fail! You can't win by blindly following the competition. Good for you for taking a fresh look at your pricing.

Summarize your pricing decisions on the Budget. If you have decided to add new products or services, make adjustments to your budget for sales and expenses. Put the form in your *Biz Plan Binder*.

This is the budgeting process: Set Goals, play the game, keep score, make decisions based on the score, change you behaviors, revise your Goals, play the game again.

Spend up to three hours today on budgeting. Print up the Excel form and store your work in your *Biz Plan Binder*.

....

TIP: Bottom line…if you want to make more money, raising your Selling Prices is a great idea. Go for it! Tomorrow, we'll explore ways to help you find new customers and sell at higher prices. So, relax and notch those prices up a bit more!

Wrap up by 5 pm.

If you want, you can revisit the other Biz Plan exercises of the day. However, don't obsess over what you have done. It's all good! Do honor and recognize what you have accomplished. Most folks spend their lives reacting and living out others' plans. And, no matter what, wrap up by 5 pm.

Today you have taken giant steps, living the life you want to live. Thought begets reality and today's thoughts and actions have already altered the course of your life. Your Biz Plan and business are powerful ways to express your creativity.

Extra credit!

Take a trip to a great bookstore this evening. Visit the travel section. What destinations appeal to you? Find a book on beauty or fashion and consider what you would like to do to look your best. Go to the biographies and notice who you would like to meet and spend time with. Check out the home and gardens section. What do you want your surroundings to look and feel like? In the spirituality and philosophy sections, consider what kinds of study you would like to explore.

Bottom line: Honor what feels good to you. Pay attention to what stirs your soul. If you could live your life your way on your terms – and you can! – what would that life BE like? Look for inspiration in the bookstore. Have fun imagining everything you want coming to you.

Have a light dinner at the bookstore. Or, eat some fresh, healthy food at home. If you like, watch a funny movie or something inspirational…but avoid news, TV commercials and anything that may interrupt the Perfect Life you are living. At least for today and tomorrow.

Off to bed.

Go through the meditation exercise like you did last night. Practice shutting your thoughts off as you slip into revitalizing sleep. If you wake in the middle of the night, discipline yourself to let the thoughts go…and relax back into sleep.

If you struggle with sleeping through the night, this is a good opportunity to try these suggestions. You can learn how to relax and sleep. Let this be yet another area in which your Perfect Life can manifest.

"To sleep, perchance to dream."

~ William Shakespeare

Lights out by 10:30.

SUNDAY

6:30 a.m. – Follow yesterday's "Rise and Shine" routine. Get started in a powerful, positive way and embrace Day Two of the *Weekend Biz Plan*!

"Learn how to be happy with what you have while you pursue all that you want."

~ Jim Rohn

TIP: Is an important part of your weekend attending church services? Great! Restructure the time frame to work with your time of worship.

7:30 A.M.

2 Hours on the Marketing Plan

Marketing is how you get the message out to the right people about what you have to offer. Good marketing results in a "reach" in your direction: A call or a website hit or a visit to your retail store. Here are the Bare-Bones Basics of the Marketing Process:

- ⊙ **Assemble ideas.** List ways to market and publicize your business on your Master To-Do List.

- ⊙ **Refine your Target Market.** Explore who really wants or needs what you are offering.

- ⊙ **Research expenses.** Find out what it costs for Yellow Pages ads, radio, billboards, TV, newspaper, classified ads, printing services, etc., for prospective marketing vehicles.

- ⊙ **Research your competitors.** Discover what they do well and poorly. Find out what they offer and how much they charge. Look for ways to be better, cleaner, nicer, smarter, faster, and more polite.

- ⊙ **Review and revise your budget.** Assess your actual sales and expenses to budget. Adjust your budget and your marketing efforts for the best effect with the fewest dollars.

- ⊙ **Assemble the Marketing Summary.** Assign marketing vehicles. Commit to putting dates on your Calendar to prepare and launch your chosen marketing vehicles.

- ⊙ **Create your marketing vehicles.** Coordinate efforts with graphic artists, advertising sales representatives and printing companies. Check for USP, consistency in brand.

41

- **Launch your marketing vehicles.** Make sure they get out into the marketplace.
- **Leverage your marketing efforts with publicity.** Get positive attention for your company on the basis of your USP, your personality, your good deeds in the community.
- **Assess your marketing efforts.** Keep track of the results. Do more of what works and less of what doesn't.
- **Repeat the process.**

As a business owner, you are always marketing. And if you plan to share your business plan with an investor or partner, they are going to want to see what you are going to do to find customers and get their attention. This weekend, we are simply going to get the ball rolling.

The Marketing Summary is the required piece for staying on track with the *Weekend Biz Plan.* Find the form called Marketing Summary at www.barebonesbiz.com/weekend As you progress with your business, you can fill in the columns concerned with performance. For starters, fill in the Marketing Vehicles, when you are going to launch them, and how much you will spend. Refer to your Budget and "tweak" it as needed.

Marketing Summary Exercise

You can use iCalendar or Outlook to incorporate your marketing efforts. The point is to commit to some action – on specific days – that will help you create a "reach" for your products and services.

Take note of the dollar amount you have in your Budget for Marketing. Now, spend 90 minutes filling out the Marketing Summary and updating your Calendar. It's an engineering challenge...how to best use your marketing dollars for maximum effect. Note that you will check your successes by updating the Marketing Summary every week.

☐ Review the Marketing Process above and commit to Marketing vehicles that you can launch.

There is much more to learn about marketing. However, fortunes were built on systems as simple as this: Block out some time to go door to door or business to business and introduce yourself. Hand out a business card or a flyer, share your Elevator Speech and ask your prospective clients what's driving them crazy. You may be able to help them out. For the *Weekend Biz Plan*, do at least this…and whatever else you choose to put on the Calendar.

Work on your Marketing Summary and Calendar until 9:30 am.

"What is now proved was once only imagined."

~ William Blake

TIP: There's lots more to learn about Marketing and Sales… and lots to DO to get the phone ringing and sales soaring The Weekend Biz Plan is designed to help you think new thoughts and engage in new actions to create better results. Next exercise, we'll assemble a list of Top Projects so that you can fill in the gaps in your Biz Plan…and your business!

Have a light snack and go outside. Go for a brisk walk or just experience the weather. A change of scenery can recharge your batteries. Take a dozen deep breaths and exhale…Ahhhhhh.

Bonus! If you meet someone while you are outside walking or experiencing the weather, say, "Hello!" and give them your Elevator Speech. Then, ask, "So what do you do?"

Back to Biz Planning at 10:00 am…

"They say things happen for a reason…
You don't do them, they won't."

~ Donavon Frankenreiter, American music artist

10 A.M.

2.5 Hours to Define Top Projects

Next up: What projects can you commit to that will get this business go go going.? A project is a set of "to-dos" that solve a problem or capture an opportunity. It's time to assemble your Top Projects list.

Before we do, let's pause for a brief overview of your Plan Binder to help you see how the work you have been doing in The *Weekend Biz Plan* is helping you build a successful business.

Business guru Stephen Covey says, "Begin with the end in mind." That's why you started this adventure by describing your Perfect Life and developing your Mission Statement. Then, you identified your USP and created your Elevator Speech.

Next, I asked you to write down your Goals. Goals are the milestones in the pursuit of your Mission and your Perfect Life. You created the Organization Chart to help you start Building Your Team. You developed your Budget to support your financial Goals and create a reasonable Selling Price. You spent time considering how to get the phone to ring and crafted your Marketing Calendar.
Note how the sections flow from one to the other. Each section of your Biz Plan supports the whole.

Now, it's time to focus on action. What should you do NOW to achieve your Goals?

Top Projects List Exercise

Find the Top Projects form at www.barebonesbiz.com/weekend The Top Projects List can help you get things done and keep you from being overwhelmed. Look over the your Goals. Review your Budget. What actions, projects, to do's will help you accomplish those Goals? Assemble no more than 10 Projects that will get your attention and commitment over the next few months.

What should your Top Projects be? Jot down as many projects as you can on your Master To-Do List. Review each one by asking: Is this moving us toward our Goals? Is this project helping us make more sales and profits? Is this the best use of our time and energy at this moment?

Examples of Top Projects can be…

- Find a mentor – someone who owns a successful company similar to mine in a different market – and "befriend" him or her.
- Complete your Marketing Plan and Calendar for the next six months.
- Create your Position Descriptions.
- Find and participate in a Sales Training course.
- Develop an Operations Manual.
- Learn to use the Accounting system and get to a Known Financial Position.
- Play with different budgeting assumptions and create your 1st, 2nd, and 3rd year budgets.
- Create a Sales Scorecard.
- Develop a Price Book or Price Menu based on the budget.
- Read *Where Did the Money Go?* by Ellen Rohr, and review it with your team and acccountant.

Put no more than 10 projects on the Top Projects list. For another project to make it to the Top Projects list, one project has to get done and moved off the list. Store a copy of your Top Projects list in your *Biz Plan Binder*.

The best part about the Top Project List? It helps you move out of overwhelm and into focused action. It's a nice feeling!

The Master To-Do List Exercise

By now, you may have considered a lot of great projects that need to get done. And you can't do everything all at once. What doesn't make it to the Top Projects list stays on the Master To-Do list. This is where you will keep everything that needs to be written down until you find a better place for it…like on your Calendar or on the Top Projects list as something else gets done.

Wrap up this exercise by 12:30.

BREAK FOR LUNCH

Enjoy a quick, healthy lunch. Review your *Biz Plan Binder* as you do. Yesterday, you had a bright idea. Today…you have a profitable business plan! You have moved thoughts to reality and your are holding it in your hands. Cool, huh? Allow yourself to get excited about this business!

"The future never just happened. It was created."

~ Will Durant

1 P. M.

One Hour to Write the Executive Summary

On one page, answer these vital questions:

- What do you do? (Elevator Speech)
- Why? (Mission)
- For whom? (Target Market)
- How are you going to get them to want what you offer? (Marketing Summary)
- What are your Goals? (Goals)
- How do you make money? (Budget)
- Who else does this? (Describe your competition)
- What makes you better? (USP)

The Executive Summary is a standard component of all business plans. It's sometimes called the one-page business plan. The work you have done this weekend has prepared you for this exercise. Review the previous exercises. Read through the pages in your *Biz Plan Binder*. Find and correct any inconsistencies. Can you see how your business is beginning to take shape?

Now, let's suppose you are an admirer of Warren Buffet, one of the world's smartest and most successful businesspeople. Imagine that you meet him at a seminar, a cocktail party or...in an elevator. You introduce yourself with your Elevator Speech. And Warren says, "That's interesting. Tell me more."

That's where the Executive Summary comes in. Your Elevator Speech is the 25-second summary of your business. Your Executive Summary is the 2-minute version.

In response to Warren's request to "tell me more," you could share your Executive Summary. Recite the main points and hand him a written copy.

Find the form called Executive Summary at www.barebonesbiz.com/weekend Craft a summary of your business, and keep it to one page. Longer than that and you are wasting words. Brevity is clarity. Write your Executive Summary and add it to your *Biz Plan Binder*.

Ta da! You did it! You have a business plan. You have clarified your vision and crafted a plan of action for helping you get there. Woohoooo! Congratulations!

Let's go back to meeting Warren Buffet. Imagine that Warren is impressed with your Executive Summary and offers to meet with you for an hour in his office to go over your business plan. You accept his offer.

You bring your *Biz Plan Binder* to the meeting. You flip through it, section by section. You share your business ideas and how you intend to move forward. You answer his questions and ask him a few of your own. Then, just imagine when Warren offers to…

- ⊙ Buy your company for multiples of millions of dollars.
- ⊙ Be on your board of advisors.
- ⊙ Introduce you to just the right person who can help you reach one of your Goals.
- ⊙ Whatever you imagine!
  Fill in the blank:_____.

See how it fits together? This weekend, you created your business plan. It's a trail map of an unknown world: your business empire. You are creating that world as you go. By thinking, gaining clarity, and intensifying your intention. Then, by taking inspired, exciting action in the direction of what you want. You'll measure results and assess your progress. You can always change your tactics…and keep your eyes focused on the horizon. Your *Biz Plan Binder* is a foundation on which you can build a rockin' business and your Perfect Life.

One more thing. It's not achieving Goals that create joy and wealth. It's choosing to be joyful…now. It's realizing that you are already wealthy and being grateful…now. Business is about playing an honorable, satisfying, stimulating, creative game and using each day to express your Mission and purpose. And the Goal getting is just icing on the cake.

And like any adventure, there will be challenging moments. Press on! I promise you this: You and your business and the world are the better for having a vision and a plan. Congratulations!

TIP: Here's an idea to help you with your Executive Summary. Answer the basic "Journalist" questions. These are questions media folks use when they are nailing down a story. What? Why? Who? By When? For Whom? How Much? How? Have fun putting your Biz Plan into a single page. This exercise helps you gain clarity. With clarity and intention you will always figure out the "How."

QUICK BREAK AND BRAG...

Go somewhere and shout as loud as you can, "I have a dream and a PLAN!" Stretch! Take a few deep breaths. Shake it out.

Now, it's time to brag on what you've done. Find someone to share your business plan with. Be selective. This must be someone who will unconditionally acknowledge what you have done and applaud. There will be time for criticism...tomorrow or the next day. You can present your *Biz Plan Binder* to another savvy business owner or mentor. You can ask that person to share thoughts for "plusing" and improving the plan.

But not today. Today, call one person and totally brag on yourself for a job well done. Lay your Elevator Speech on them. Read your Executive Summary. Bask in the glory. Show them what you have been working on. Let them know that you are committed to expanding peace, prosperity and freedom through your own successful business.

Your rockin' *Weekend Biz Plan* is just the beginning!

Back to work! You are on the final stretch!

2:30 P.M.

1.5 hours to Your Regular Meeting With YOU

Grab your Calendar...Outook or iCalendar or an old school appointment book. Make a standing appointment with yourself to review and update your *Biz Plan Binder* and plan your time. Pick an hour on Sunday night or Monday morning, before the work week begins. Commit to this meeting, starting today, and every week from here on. Whether you are just getting started in business or you are the CEO of a mega-millions empire, this meeting with yourself is the most important moment of the week.

Spend an hour now reviewing your business plan and organizing your upcoming week. Flip through your *Biz Plan Binder*. Read over your Perfect Life for inspiration. Look over your Mission. See yourself achieving your Goals. Look over the Marketing Summary. Review the Top Projects List and the Master To-Do List. Edit and refine your business plan.

Ask yourself, "This week, what is the BEST use of my time? What will help me live my Perfect Life, fulfill my Mission and move me towards my Goals?"

Your time is infinitely valuable. Invest it wisely. Don't squander it. Time management guru Dan Sullivan says, "You can have everything you love in life as long as you give up things you hate."

Don't do things you hate. Don't hang out with people who suck the life out of you. You are too smart for that! Life is too precious.

Commit your time to things that make you happy with people you love, do things that move you to your Goals and allow you to express your greatest gifts.

Plan your week.

Block out family time first. Look ahead for upcoming travel and

	Monday, Aug 16	Tuesday, Aug 17	Wednesday, Aug 18	Thursday, Aug 19	Friday, Aug 20	Saturday, Aug 21	Sunday, Aug
6 am	Coffee, news						
7 00	Meeting with ME - plan week, update business	Coffee, news / Meet with Jeff	Coffee, news / Meet with Bill	Coffee, news / Meet with Stacy	Coffee, news		
8 00	Check Scorecards, Dispatch Cleaning Techs	Sales and Service Meeting - All Plumbers	Check Scorecards, Dispatch Cleaning Techs	Check Scorecards, Dispatch Cleaning Techs	Check Scorecards, Dispatch Cleaning Techs		
9 00	Work with Sue on Financials, Payroll	Dispatch Cleaning Techs		Ride Along with Stacy - lunch on the road. Write 10 point Checklist for Water Heater replacements. Role Play the Sales Steps.		T-Ball game!	
10 00							
11 00							Church
12 pm	Lunch	Lunch	Lunch		Lunch		
1 00	Update Price Book	Financial Quick Check Meeting - Bean Team	Marketing - work on Direct Mail campaign		Marketing - finish YP ads, update Marketing Budget		Golf
2 00							
3 00							
4 00	Enter AP / Email, phone calls	Enter AP / Email, phone calls	Enter AP / Email, phone calls	Enter AP / Email, phone calls	Enter AP / Email, phone calls		
5 00	Workout, Meditate and Spanish!	Workout, Meditate and Spanish!	Workout, Meditate and Spanish!	Workout, Meditate and Spanish!	Workout, Meditate and Spanish!	Workout, Meditate and Spanish!	Workout, Meditate Spanish!
6 00							

meetings. Schedule time to fulfill the responsibilities for each Position you hold on the Organization Chart. Block out time to work on your Marketing and Top Projects. Schedule time for rest, relaxation, exercise and play! Here's a sample Calendar put together by the owner of a Plumbing company. What you choose to do is up to you. Do plan your time…or risk be planned for by others. Pack a tight Calendar.

4 P.M.

Celebrate!

That's it! Page through your *Biz Plan Binder*. Take another look at your Calendar. Yes, things will change once the week begins. You can always change the day to day Calendar appointments. Still, you've got a PLAN. Work the Plan and punt when you must.

It's the end of the weekend and the beginning of your successful business. Congratulations! Go forth and prosper! Do whatever you want to do for the rest of the evening. You are ready to hit the ground running on Monday morning!

MONDAY MORNING!

It's time to get into action. You may be building a business part time while you continue to work at your job. Or, last Friday, you may have told your boss what to do with that dead-end job you walked out on! Maybe you are returning to a business that you started some time ago. In any event, you now have a Plan. You have blocked out your Calendar with actions that will move you towards your dreams. Go for it!

Today, at the end of the day, take 15 minutes and reflect on how you did. Your Biz Plan and your Calendar need to be flexible as well as focused. You might have to move something that you didn't get to. It's all good. Life happens. Adjust the Calendar. Tomorrow's another day. Just keep moving in the direction of your dreams.

Once a week, have the Meeting with You. Review your Biz Plan. Take note of each section. Be inspired by your Perfect Life essay.

Make note of any progress you've made towards your Goals. Check your actual financial performance against your Budget. Update your Top Projects list. Just keep enhancing and refining the Biz Plan. Just keep thinking, planning and moving in the direction of your dreams.

This Biz Plan may be all you need to create the business–and life –of your dreams. If you would like to explore more on business planning, visit www.barebonesbiz.com And, check out The Bare Bones Biz Plan. This six-week business planning program may be a good next step for you...to help you build on the basic Weekend Biz Plan. We also have personalized consulting if you want specific one-to-one business building consulting.

WE ARE HERE TO HELP...A LITTLE OR A LOT AS DESIRED OR REQUIRED. SO, STAY IN TOUCH KEEP COMING BACK... TO WWW.BAREBONESBIZ.COM!

You've put together your *Biz Plan Binder*. You've spent the weekend clarifying your vision and committing to an action plan that will take you in the direction of your dreams. Job well done.

I want to hear from you! Contact me to share your experience. You will be greeted with appreciation and wild applause. And, keep checking in at www.barebonesbiz.com Sign up for our free ezine, the Bare Bones Biz Expose. It's chock full of biz tips, video role plays and solid systems for growing a profitable business and send your questions and success stories to us at contact@barebonesbiz.com. Our Mission: to expand peace, prosperity and freedom!

xoxo

"To do what you love and feel that it matters – what could be more fun?"

~ Katharine Graham

WHAT IF I DON'T FINISH MY BIZ PLAN IN ONE WEEKEND? AND OTHER FREQUENTLY ASKED QUESTIONS...

What if I don't finish my Biz Plan in one weekend?

The main thing is to get started. Benjamin Franklin said," A job begun is half done." He was right! If you got your Biz Plan started you are off and running. Schedule time in the upcoming weeks to continue working on the Biz Plan.

Over the course of the weekend, is it better to finish one exercise before moving on to the next?

I built in time limits for two reasons. One, your first swing at an exercise is often the best one. Don't over think the exercises. Allow yourself to be inspired and go with what first comes to mind. And, when the time is up, stop working on that exercise and move to the next. You can – and should – revisit your Biz Plan. I suggest you review your Biz Plan at least once a week, during the Meeting with You.

I have a partner. Should we work on the Weekend Biz Plan together?

Great idea! Do the Perfect Life Exercise separately. Then, compare your essays. Are you aligned? Then, work on the rest of the exercises together.

Note that you may need to spend more time. together to work through the Biz Plan. Maybe schedule another weekend?

And, if your partner won't commit to the Biz Plan, I encourage you to do one anyway. Then, show your partner your Biz Plan and see if you can find agreement and common ground. Unless you both share the same vision for your company, you may be heading for a breakdown in your business or your relationship. A Biz Plan can help you get you back on track!

SPECIAL THANKS TO...

The Bare Bones Biz Team...Gail, Shauna, Michelle and Jon. Here's to the breakthrough! Xo$

ABOUT BARE BONES BIZ AND AUTHOR ELLEN ROHR

I almost sunk our family business. I assumed I knew enough about business to run a dinky little plumbing company. After all, I had spent about $100,000 of my parents' money on my college degree in Business Administration. In fact, I graduated at the top of my class. Still, I didn't know how to balance a checkbook!

I got involved in my husband's company after his partner died unexpectedly. Boy, was I humbled! It seemed like lots of money was moving through the company, but at the end of the month there was never any money left. Thankfully, I found a mentor, a savvy plumbing contractor. Frank Blau wrote a column in *Plumbing & Mechanical* magazine. I wrote to him and asked for help. He took me under his wing and taught me how to keep score in business. He taught me how to read and use financial reports. He taught me how to make money.

We turned our company around. We paid off our business loan. We doubled sales and tripled the amount of money we took out of the company. Very cool. My husband and I went middle-age crazy. We sold the company to our employees–a friendly coup d'etat!–and bought a gentleman's farm in the country. (Picture "Green Acres.") At this point, I realized that I wanted to share what I'd learned. After all, if a smart, highly educated person like me didn't know how to read a Balance Sheet, I figured business illiteracy must be rampant. I was right.

My experiences since then have included teaching and consulting with hundreds of small businesses, primarily plumbing and heating companies. In my seminars, I rarely find a student who creates and reads financial statements on a regular basis, much less uses financial information to make management decisions. In fact, few know their assets from their liabilities!

I started Bare Bones Biz – a training and consulting company – to teach folks how to turn their big ideas into successful businesses. I teach the basics, the simple disciplines that can take your company from flab to fit. I've written two books on business basics, *Where Did the Money Go? – Accounting Basics for the Business Owner Who Wants to Get Profitable,* and *How Much Should I Charge? – Pricing Basics for Making Money Doing What You Love.*

My consulting work led to a position as president of Benjamin Franklin Plumbing, a home-service plumbing franchise company. We grew from zero to $40 million in franchise sales, the 18th-fastest growing franchise in 2003. I learned a lot about what works to grow fast and profitably...and what doesn't. Guess what! The basics never go out of style, no matter how big a company gets.

This book, *The Weekend Biz Plan,* is an essential part of my plan to help improve business literacy. It ties into my website, www.barebonesbiz.com, THE community for BASIC business information.

You can also check out *The Bare Bones Biz Plan. The Weekend Biz Plan* will get your started (or jump started!) The Bare Bones Biz Plan is an intensive Six-Week business planning and "turnaround" system if you want to keep go go going! It's like taking a fitness class or committing to a full basic training workout camp. We are here to help... however you choose to make changes in your life. Together, we can build extraordinary businesses and expand World Peace.

TELL US YOUR BIZ SUCCESS STORY!

The Bare Bones Biz Team
contact@barebonesbiz.com
www.barebonesbiz.com
877.629.7647
417.753.3685 fax
3120 S. Know It All Lane
Rogersville, MO 65742

I wish you love, peace and lots of money!

xoxo$

Made in the USA
Columbia, SC
06 July 2021